W9-CIA-988

Pioneer Spirit
The
Westward
Expansion

THE TRANSCONTINENTAL RAILROAD

Rachel Lynette

PowerKiDS press™

New York

For Adam

Published in 2014 by The Rosen Publishing Group, Inc.
29 East 21st Street, New York, NY 10010

First Edition

Editor: Jennifer Way
Book Design: Greg Tucker

Photo Credits: Cover, p. 21 © Architect of the Capitol/EverGreene Painting Studios; p. 5 Underwood Archives/Archive Photos/Getty Images; p. 6 Matt Meadows/Peter Arnold/Getty Images; p. 7 De Agostini Picture Library/Getty Images; p. 8 Library of Congress; p. 10 Kean Collection/Archive Photos/Getty Images; pp. 11, 17, 19 Universal Images Group/Getty Images; p. 12 Hulton Archives/Stringer/Getty Images; pp. 13, 15 MPI/Stringer/Archive Photos/Getty Images; p. 16 Matt Grant/Shutterstock.com; p. 18 Robert Nickelsberg/Getty Images News/Getty Images; p. 22 Steve Heap/Shutterstock.com.

Library of Congress Cataloging-in-Publication Data

Lynette, Rachel.
  The transcontinental railroad / by Rachel Lynette. — First edition.
     pages cm. — (Pioneer spirit: the westward expansion)
  Includes index.
  ISBN 978-1-4777-0785-2 (library binding) — ISBN 978-1-4777-0903-0 (pbk.) —
ISBN 978-1-4777-0904-7 (6-pack)
  1. Pacific railroads—History—Juvenile literature. 2. Railroads—United States—History—Juvenile literature. 3. Railroads—West (U.S.)—History—Juvenile literature. I. Title.
  TF25.P23L96 2014
  385.0978—dc23
                              2012050205

Manufactured in the United States of America

CPSIA Compliance Information: Batch #S13PK5: For Further Information contact Rosen Publishing, New York, New York at 1-800-237-9932

CONTENTS

Across the West

The Transcontinental Railroad was the first set of railroad tracks to stretch across the western United States. It was also the biggest and most expensive construction project of the 1800s. It took six years and thousands of workers to complete.

The Transcontinental Railroad played a big role in the **westward expansion**. The westward expansion was the movement of people from the eastern part of the United States to the West. Millions of people traveled on the Transcontinental Railroad to settle in the West. It made what had once been a long and dangerous trip easier, safer, and much faster.

These covered wagons are passing a train that is moving along newly laid Transcontinental Railroad tracks. Train travel overtook wagon travel after this railroad was completed.

A Difficult Journey

In the early 1800s, many people in the United States wanted to travel or settle out West. Traveling long distances was not easy back then. People traveling over land had to walk, ride horses, or travel in covered wagons. A journey out West could take four months or even longer. There was also no way to move heavy goods such as coal, iron, or livestock without floating them down rivers on boats.

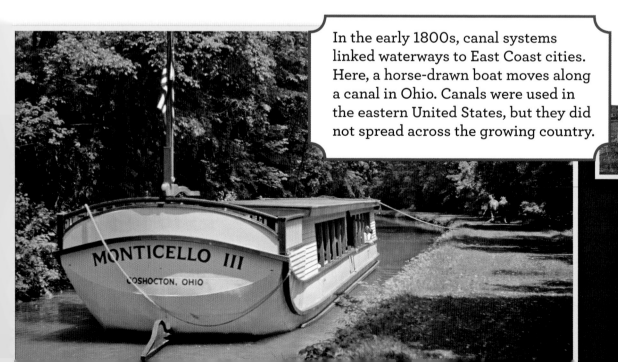

In the early 1800s, canal systems linked waterways to East Coast cities. Here, a horse-drawn boat moves along a canal in Ohio. Canals were used in the eastern United States, but they did not spread across the growing country.

MONTICELLO III
COSHOCTON, OHIO

Before the Transcontinental Railroad was built, people made the months-long journey west in covered wagons, like the ones in this painting.

In 1825, the first **steam engine** train was invented in England. It could carry heavy **freight**. People in the United States saw that railroads could be used to quickly and safely move freight and people across the country.

Choosing a Route

By the 1850s, railroads were being used in the eastern United States. Teams of **engineers** were sent west to plan routes for a railroad that would go west across the country. The biggest challenge they faced in planning a route was finding a way to cross the Sierra Nevada Mountains.

Abraham Linc[o]

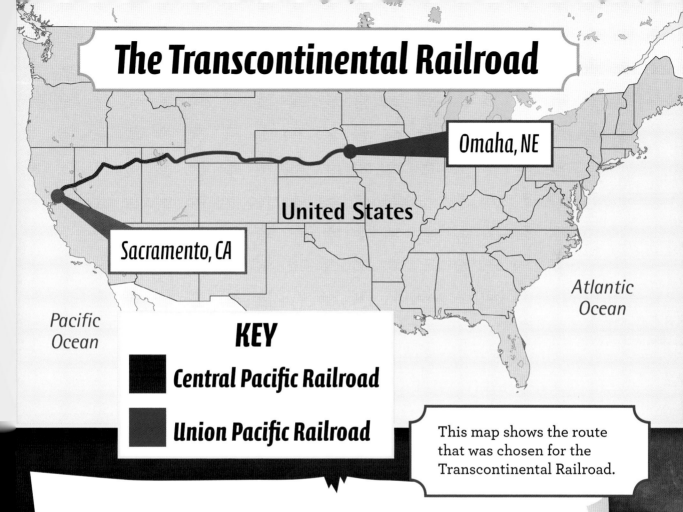

The Transcontinental Railroad

Omaha, NE

United States

Sacramento, CA

Pacific
Ocean

Atlantic
Ocean

KEY

Central Pacific Railroad

Union Pacific Railroad

This map shows the route that was chosen for the Transcontinental Railroad.

A route was chosen soon after the **Civil War** began in 1861. Eleven Southern states had **seceded** from the nation at the beginning of the war. Because of this, the Transcontinental Railroad's route went through the states and territories that remained part of the Union. On July 1, 1862, President Abraham Lincoln signed the Pacific Railway Act.

From the East and the West

Two companies were chosen to build the railroad. In 1863, the Central Pacific Railroad started building eastward from Sacramento, California. Its big challenge was to get through the Sierra Nevada Mountains. It also had a hard time getting supplies because the supplies they needed had to be shipped from the East.

The Union Pacific Railroad began construction moving westward from Omaha, Nebraska Territory, in 1865.

Grenville Dodge was a major general in the Union army during the Civil War. After the war ended, he became the chief engineer of the Union Pacific Railroad. He helped plan the Transcontinental Railroad's route.

Grenville Dodge found a pass for the railroad through the Black Hills in South Dakota and Wyoming. Many parts of the railroad's route would need to have tunnels or bridges built, though.

The Union Pacific Railroad started construction later because it had trouble finding workers until after the Civil War ended.

The plan was for the two companies to meet and join their tracks. The companies raced to see who could lay the most track.

Working on the Railroad

Railway men worked for twelve hours a day, six days a week. They had to clear dirt and rocks, carry heavy wooden ties and steel rails, and pound stakes into the ground with sledgehammers. In the West, there were freezing temperatures, blizzards, and **avalanches**. Workers had to use dangerous **explosives** to blast tunnels through solid rock. Men were injured or killed while doing this dangerous work.

The Devil's Gate Bridge, shown here, was built to cross Weber Canyon in Utah.

Here are workers on the Union Pacific Railroad standing in front of wagon bearing supplies for construction.

In the East, the land was flat, but there were challenges and dangers. In the Great Plains, workers had to build bridges across many rivers. Workers also had to lay tracks through deserts where temperatures could reach 110° F (43° C).

Immigrant Labor

At first most of the men working for the Central Pacific Railroad in the West were Irish **immigrants**. By the time they reached the mountains, many of these workers quit due to the harsh working conditions. The railroad began to hire Chinese workers. Many of these Chinese immigrants had come to California during the **Gold Rush**. Eventually, around 80 percent of Central Pacific workers were Chinese.

The Chinese immigrants proved to be hard workers. Many also knew how to work with explosives. The Chinese workers were given the hardest and most dangerous jobs. They were often treated unfairly. For example, Chinese workers were paid less than white workers.

Chinese railroad workers worked alongside white workers, but faced prejudice and unequal pay. They protested unsuccessfully for equal wages.

Native Americans and the Railroad

The Union Pacific Railroad laid track through the plains where Native Americans had been living for thousands of years. Workers killed the buffalo that the Plains Native Americans hunted for food. The Native Americans knew that the railroad would bring more settlers to their land.

The Plains Native Americans fought back. They destroyed tracks and attacked workers. In 1867, a group of Native Americans overturned a **handcar**.

A handcar is a hand-powered rail cart used by railroad workers.

Native Americans fought against the expansion of railroads in the West while they were being built, as well as afterward. This picture shows Native Americans attacking a Union Pacific train in 1870.

Only one member of the railroad crew survived. The US government sent soldiers to protect the railroad workers. The soldiers killed many Native Americans. They forced many more to leave their land and moved them to **reservations**.

Towns Along the Track

As the tracks moved west, towns sprung up almost overnight. Stores, **saloons**, **gambling** houses, and dance halls opened in quickly constructed buildings. When the workers had time off, they spent their time and money in these towns. Gambling, stealing, cheating, and even shootings were common.

The city of Cheyenne, Wyoming, got its start as a town along the Transcontinental Railroad. Today it is the capital of the state.

SQUARE MEALS
LODGINGS

RICHEST MINING
REGION

This picture shows a busy new station that has popped up along a newly laid railroad.

Most of these towns were abandoned as soon as workers moved on to build a new part of the track. Business owners followed the workers. However, some towns became stops along the railroad and attracted new settlers. The city of Cheyenne, Wyoming, was founded by the Union Pacific Railroad and has since become the biggest city in the state.

The Golden Spike

In the spring of 1869, both of the railroad companies were racing toward Promontory Summit in the Utah Territory. This was where the two tracks would meet. On April 28, workers from the Central Pacific Railroad set a record by laying more than 10 miles (16 km) of track in a single day!

On May 10, 1869, a ceremony was held to join the two tracks. More than 500 people, including railroad officials and newspaper reporters, were there to see the event. A golden spike was pounded into the final rail to complete the track. The Transcontinental Railroad was completed!

This painting shows the ceremony where the Union Pacific Railroad and the Central Pacific Railroad met at Promontory Summit, Utah.

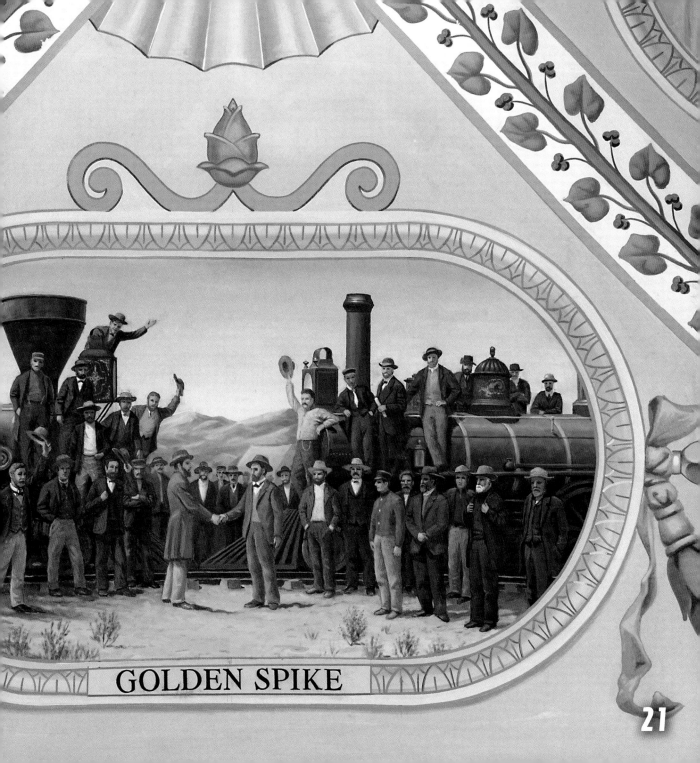

GOLDEN SPIKE

Taking the Train

The Transcontinental Railroad brought millions of people west to settle on the land. A trip from New York to California that once took six months or longer could be made in just seven days!

Many of the new settlers were farmers who had been granted land from the government or people who started businesses. The railroad also carried goods and mail across the country. By making long distance travel easier and faster, the Transcontinental Railroad played an important part in westward expansion.

The growth of railroads helped speed up the westward expansion in the last part of the nineteenth century. Some railroad lines are still in use today. Others, like the one shown here, are used to give tourists rides along historic routes.

GLOSSARY

avalanches (A-vuh-lanch-ez) When a large amounts of snow, ice, earth, or dirt slide down a mountainside.

Civil War (SIH-vul WOR) The war fought between the Northern and the Southern states of America from 1861 to 1865.

engineers (en-juh-NEERZ) People who are masters at planning and building engines, machines, roads, and bridges.

explosives (ek-SPLOH-sives) Things that can explode.

freight (FRAYT) The goods that a train, boat, or airplane carries.

gambling (GAM-bul-ing) Betting money on the result of something.

Gold Rush (GOHLD RUSH) A time in the mid-1800s when people found gold in the ground in California.

handcar (HAND-kar) A hand-powered rail cart used by railroad workers.

immigrants (IH-muh-gruntz) People who moves to a new country from another country.

reservations (reh-zer-VAY-shunz) Areas of land set aside by the government for Native Americans to live on.

saloons (suh-LOONZ) Places for eating, drinking, and playing games. Saloons often rented rooms and held poker games for guests.

seceded (sih-SEED-id) To have withdrawn from a group or a country.

steam engine (STEEM EN-jun) An engine powered by steam.

westward expansion (WES-twurd ik-SPANT-shun) The continued growth of the United States by adding land to the west and having settlers

INDEX

WEBSITES

Due to the changing nature of Internet links, PowerKids Press has developed an online list of websites related to the subject of this book. This site is updated regularly. Please use this link to access the list:
www.powerkidslinks.com/pswe/rail/